City Slicker

encounters with the outside

Stephanie Barbé Hammer

BAMBOO DART PRESS

LOS ANGELES † NEW YORK † LONDON † MELBOURNE

City Slicker: encounters with the outside by Stephanie Barbé Hammer
ISBN: 978-1-947240-51-3
eISBN: 978-1-947240-52-0

Cover artwork by Dennis Callaci

Chapbook design and layout by Mark Givens

For information:
Bamboo Dart Press
chapbooks@bamboodartpress.com

Bamboo Dart Press 022

www.pelekinesis.com

www.bamboodartpress.com

www.shrimperrecords.com

For Bonnie Hearn Hill

CONTENTS

67th street entrance, central park, 1958
(new york city)

the path off the big avenue with buses and taxis leads through an opening in a stone wall, past silent soldiers in bronze statue stillness, into an immense garden and in that garden is the playground. beyond that, are rocks and lawns and benches and the zoo entrance where the seals swim in their own private pond.

but let's pause at the playground where all the friends are. the playground friends who are friends just because you see them every day. it's that easy.

now stop.

sit in the sandbox with suzannah and wait for the man in green to come with his long metal wand to turn on the rain that springs from the metal post in the middle of the cement. he twists a screw or a bolt or a spigot or a bib or a wheel handle (that's it!), and the rain comes. you will run in and out of this middle of the hot playground cold shower. not like something called a swimming pool, which you have not seen yet. that is thing people have in the country. but here in the city in the park in the playground there is spray that sputters shoots out and splats on pavement.

you dart around those droplets, screaming with surprise-shivers along with suzannah and della and the other kids including a girl who speaks only french, but it doesn't matter, because playing is communication.

wait.

the ice-cream man comes with his cart, and maybe your father too if it is a saturday, and you slurp the sweet on a stick that your mother gives you, and then you run back because suzannah calls you into this magic circle, where you clap your hands and pretend they're flippers, and you imagine being a creature always wet and always moving like water in the distance the sound of cars.

outside alone at night for the first time, 1959
(seattle, washington)

on a swing. alone because
the cousin has gone inside
for some reason. she is my only
relative who is my age that
i know about and i trust her
because she knows about grass
and going barefoot. i point my toes
to go up on the swing. lean back
she showed me this. and then i carefully
jump off... a skill i just learned.
i have never seen night come in over
houses, til now. the grass grows cold
under my feet and there are the sounds of
other children playing in other yards.
a star, two stars. then the older cousin
— the mother of the one i was just talking about —
calls me.
i linger and wonder what it would be like to
play outside all the time and to never wear
shoes to see time pass in the sky
and to have neighbors
so that i can be by myself
but at the same time
be accompanied.

night in 5, 1959

(fire island, new york)

there are no stars in
new york city; the
sky is black because
the buildings tower up
windows of whiteness
so try: imagine
stars seen for the first
time, coming out of a
movie with parents
on fire island — i
looked at the big sky
filled with tiny brights
scattered sparkles i
said look but they did
not see. i lonewalked
quiet. see—i knew
myself different. i
felt things they didn't.
they talked about the
movie. but i kept
watching stars all this
time making wishes
to bring back to the
city so that each
lit aperture could
become marvelous
a just discovered
shared constellation.

pinecones, 1962
(cascades, washington state)

Me
And
My dad
Walk the
Cascades in the
Woods looking for
Fallen pinecones to
Start the fire with in the cabin —
I don't wear my glasses because
They are new to me and sit strangely
On my ears, so when I pick up the thing
That is brown and mottled like a pinecone it
Just feels wrong. Pinecones are brittle and dry
This brown thing is wet and it's cold so I crouch down
To investigate with my already pretty bad eyes. A slug. I let
Go. Stand up. We walk to the stream skip tiny stones
Never minding about pinecones. But I personally never
Forget the slime-wonder of an aliveness
I thought
Was
Dead
And
Good
Only
To
Be
Burnt.

wading, 1963
(washington state)

the first time I walked into the pacific was a mistake

laughing in our corduroy pants and matching

tops my cousin and I egged each

other on to go past wading bit by bit the parents not watching

us carefully til we got

our legs soaked the cloth sticking to the skin the stain blooming

upward

the water ballooned

our underwear out from inside the sodden heavy pants

we'd started

with toes but the water was so cold and delicious and

giggling that water said let me darken those pants the water talk

won

out as water always does it felt inevitable and slow and certain so

we both

got wet past the waist and beyond to the ribs

my cousin's mom

didn't yell but she must have called us back somehow

and when

we got back to shore she

stripped us of the dripping wreck of our child apparel

stuck us in giant grown up parkas, with bandanas for panties —

why this? propriety I guess those tiny girl privates
couldn't be left naked even under a coat
our pants and tops flapped in the wind on a makeshift clothesline
we pranced in our parka dresses
waving at
the sea

ellen, 1966
(eaton center, new hampshire)

a rowboat grey and weathered setting out from a lakeshore
in new hampshire:
she sits on the bench with the oars.
we are trying to become friends
in this place where no-one is friendly.
she wears her green camp uniform and a hat.
she often wears the hat, because I think now
she must have been afraid of not being pretty
but remember how she sat across from me relaxed
determined like some people are when they are out of doors —
they're just freer, more clearly themselves.
then, she shows me how
to row.
"you just lean back and press forward and
don't forget to turn the oars so they skim the air —"
"like our arms doing the crawl ?" (— which is what we
call freestyle)
"yes," she says "like that only the wood
is the arm and it's stronger than we are — man, these are arms that can
carry us a long distance with all our stuff and food and supplies
and we'll still be dry and
ready to land for the adventure that awaits us."
she stops and we're sitting in the middle of the smooth lake.

just the two of us. There are other kids messing around with
canoes but they are far away. Years later I will
read about thoreau rhapsodizing about walden — yesterday
in fact was the first time I read it — and he talked about stillness
and I knew thanks to ellen just what
he meant.

rockefeller center, 1967
(new york city)

I never learn to figure skate will not be
one of those girls in little skirts
at the center of the rink twirling
but I learn to skate fast
my father and I go to Central Park
first and later to Rockefeller
we have our own skates we go to the
second session
when it is less crowded and colder
my father takes his coat off and puts it
in the locker
we are the first out on the rink
I skate alone for a while and then
we link arms and skate together
he is tall and I am tall so our long
legs carry us around the rink quickly
we swoop past families and couples
struggling to stay on their feet we
go and go for the whole session
no breaks
later our feet slide into shoes and feel
strange flat deflated shorn of their
wings but that's ok it's part of the magic

the return to bladeless
normalcy – then
we walk home in the Manhattan
night but first we say hello to the man with the roasted
chestnuts
cart we buy a bag and they're searing hot in
the bag my father peels them, and we eat them
walking all the way home 20 short blocks
4 long ones

I dream poems, trees, and California, 1967
(New York City)

During the winter study hall of what I will realize later is a fancy
school library off 5th Avenue
I listen to a record a classmate found of
a man reading Shakespeare sonnets to the background of guitar.
I like poetry.
I don't do homework.
I explore the shelves —
what will later be called "holdings."
I find the book
called Leaves of Grass, which is a funny title.
Grass is skinny — can it
sprout like a tree?
I sit and look out the window and weep
at the grandeur of the
the redwoods. The trees along the streets here are spindly,
bare and this man named Walt Whitman (pretty
name) writes
about arboreal giants that speak like legends.
I can't visualize them, but
I can hear them talking thanks to his book.
When I get home I tell my mother — I tell her about
all the things I read because she is the smartest
person I know and she reads everything because

she works for a company that publishes books —
"Oh him" my mother says. "he wrote this free verse stuff —
it's easier than rhythm and rhyme." "Is it?" I say.
I am already doubtful because what he wrote
seems so beautiful, and isn't beauty always hard?
Or if it isn't, isn't ease a form of genius too?
I read that book many times
in that private girls' school library wearing my
regulation navy blue uniform
wondering what it might be like to ever
sing, let alone celebrate, myself
under the canopy of giant trees.

Working a table on a street corner for Eugene McCarthy, 1968
(New York City)

I'm standing at a table on the West Side with my friend
Abby Rollins, who will die of cancer — the first one to pass
In our class at Nightingale, and we are 13 or at least not quite 14.

My father is enraged I am supporting a pacifist.

What's so stupid about wanting peace? I keep asking him
and he just says it's not realistic, **but why isn't it?** I ask
Utopia ain't, he says and I never
Understand why he isn't saying "isn't," which is
Grammatically correct and is the way we talk normally, being very
    White, and very Protestant living on the East Side, and having a
    lot of money still, or the promise of it. He thinks I'm stupid
And I think he is. My mother tells me it's
great
I'm politically involved and that seems strange too:
My Republican mother secretly against the death penalty and pro
Abortion (she had one) and pro
civil rights although she never speaks
up (maintaining what I learned recently is called "white silence")

This standing on the West Side handing out McCarthy pamphlets
is the first and last
Time for a long time that I
Believe in political things. Have hope in change. Except for
Obama and
Even when I phone-banked for him I knew he was

too conservative because what about
The war why is it always a war the war some war?
Why is peace never realistic?
Now I read about punching a Nazi, and I hate Nazis but
I can't feel glad
About it sorry. Utopia ain't. Would you like a button?
Would you like some information? I'm still standing here at this rickety card table
And I'm still wondering why peace isn't realistic. I'm just asking.
For a (dead) friend.

Bicycle, 1969
(New York City [for Leonard Hammer])

I am 15 arriving unfashionably late at this delicate party of

Hovering over two wheels — yeah, I know it's a kid's

locomotion — but we live in "the city" — no driveways no rural paths —

Now I'm desperate to learn, even as I should be learning to drive but —
again — no car.

That's when he of the renowned total impatience (remember teaching me
tennis? That fiasco of broken rackets and hurled with rage yellow balls?)

Yes, *him*. He brings

Me to the park as the Big Apple leaves begin their

Greenness; we rent the vehicle and he

Holds the back of it and says pedal

And he runs with me down the road between

The fountain and the boats. I see my

Feet moving on the black pumping rectangles. Look up he

Shouts breathless, steer, and then he lets go

That feeling of weightlessness as I leave him behind

But I hear him shouting hoarsely you've got it

You've got it.

I will never really like riding, but that

Moment of release with him waiting in the distance

For me to turn around — I will still have it 50 years later

whenever

I make something, knowing somewhere in

The background he lets go of me, still
Waits, completely attentive, beneficent, while I
Grip the handlebars, gear-crank these words.

Fog, 1972
(Northampton, Massachusetts)

Fog means sex in the mist with that boy from Bowdoin
Who plays guitar and is a genius the
Grass cold beneath bare feet, I have left
My clogs somewhere at the party house and
Forgotten where I put them and he grabs
My hand and we run across the field
In the dark. I never do things like that except
When I do, and then I do them with a
Ferocity I don't want to think about later—
Running blind til I fall on the
Ground like in some Hardy novel with a man
Who wishes me nothing but harm, but that's in
The book not how it is with this boy who
Leaves me later for another girl, and I
Get mad but I am already seeing someone else
And looking through the foggy fall turning winter the ice
Covers the branches for the next man after that who speaks
Swedish and who gives me a coffee pot for Xmas. He too
is a genius, although he cannot
Play guitar.

discomfort poem, 1974
(Paris, France)

watch this:
i have diarrhea
 in paris
and i have to walk to the *hôpital américain*
from the bus
for miles.
i have to stop every few minutes
to catch myself from spilling my insides
onto a very fancy
boulevard.
a friend is with me but we don't
know where we are going. no one
seems to understand our broken
french.
la diahrrée, i keep on saying *la diahrrée*
til we finally make it into the doctor's office
and guess what?
he's not *américain* at all
but *anglais* and he writes a
 disdainful colonial prescription
and sends us back out
to walk
to the drugstore —

we get there
it starts raining and watch this —
we just start to laugh —
i giggle carefully swallowing 4 then 6 of
Those old world *français* pills.

The Swiss guy I am seeing
Has dumped me (for the first of two times)
because
He has another American girlfriend
From my college,
Which is awkward.
I go to the Saturday night disco
At the *cité universitaire*
With a friend but either
She leaves early or she
Hooks up with someone
So when
It's time to leave
None of my friends are there
And there's no boy I'm interested in —
I walk home
By myself.
This is unthinkable in New York
But here, I'm fine.
I cross the bridge over the
Lac Léman, and see a friend
Cleaning off the tables in
The fancy restaurant where

He works as a waiter. He's illuminated
And almost alluring. There are
A few people out. The bus
Has stopped running.
The *jet d'eau* has been turned
Off.
The cafés are closed.
The streets are silent.
Rousseau hated Geneva
But I don't
Understand that.
I will never see the city
As he did – a tight
Town that
Ran like the Calvinist
Clockwork his father made.
For me Geneva will always remain
The open city where I
Walked everywhere desirous
at
Any time.

He doesn't want it, 1975
(Skåne, Sweden)

my college ex-boyfriend who is poor will end up quite rich. He'll live
in Sweden. His wife will post a video of him smiling in a cowboy hat on a
   tractor
on their farm. He grins sheepishly as though he didn't make her
film him in this obvious way — he did — But the fact is, doing farm work is

how I will remember him best. He is a brilliant sad scholarship student at an
   Ivy —
Gets into Yale grad school in German on fellowship but turns it down —
Longs to return to a farm in Skåne, where he's been an exchange student
I will take the career he declined, work my ass off because I am not and never
   will be

a genius. It'll always strike me as funny that I'm the one who becomes
the German scholar and will eventually discover that guess what? I actually
am German. But back to us: I see myself standing in Skåne hoeing sugar
   beets —

our relationship is on its last legs. It's summer. I've promised a visit so I come
after a junior year in Geneva. We break up a few months later. He is so happy
in the middle of that goddamn field. I have blisters on my hands. My back
   is killing me.

Dressed inappropriately in Ashberryian haiku, 1980
(Montpellier, France)

I'm not a hike-in-a-skirt type except for that time in Montpellier
France, which is a freak accident, but silly shit tends to happen there:
We go out for an expensive lunch with a French friend who says "let's walk!"
Suddenly there I am hiking up the *massif central* in high heels
And a dress — I feel stupid until I get to the summit and see
5 other women poised at the peak in pencil skirts and stilettos.
Boyfriend grins. I look at them and then at the view. My feet hurt. A lot.
Jean Marc says "*Magnifique!*" Boyfriend agrees. We all check out the women.
I marvel at their lipstick, mark how the red matches the napkins of
The restaurant below. I greet them. They smile, descending the slope *en pointe*.

a yellow tube top in greenwich village, 1984
(New York City [for James Schuyler])

i am trying to make this yellow tube top
work but it's
either
too short
or my
breasts are
too big
or it's just too
muggy to keep
anything up
that doesn't
have straps
so
i keep on tugging
while we sit in this
café i forget the name of
i will dine here many times
right in the heart of the
west village
with its many men
but for some
reason the time that comes to mind
is a woman — Lanie

who works with me at Rutgers:
she sips iced white wine
and eats a golden brunch
right near her apartment
which i've just seen
because
i have just moved to the village
into what will be my favorite

place that i have ever lived
from the bedroom window you can see the
empire state building if you crane forward
lean left
and when you walk outside you can see
anybody one time i walk past
lou reed sitting at the top of a stoop
and another time ballet star rudolph nureyev
sails past me in a yellow and red versace suit and
matching cap i stop on 12th street and
just stare at him
HELLO there he says
his clothes fit perfectly
although it's hot

nothing needs to be adjusted

Louis Beck drops dead, 1986
(after Tamara Madison, "drop dead")

(New York City [for Jamie Gordon])

Louis is the only person I know who actually drops dead. And he does it with panache. Walking the dog on 5th avenue outside his Central Park apartment. Manhattan. New York City.

I have always liked him. He is my college roommate's father. He takes me and my new husband out for fancy dinners. He is generous. He is one of the first people to tell people I'm Jewish, although I clearly am not. He sees my predilection for lox and tells his orthodox relatives at some brunch out on Long Island what a nice kosher girl I am.

He winks at me.

So I'm glad he gets to die standing on the street in the swankiest, WASPiest section of town, with his dog*, and his wife waiting for him upstairs. Some Egyptian artifacts tucked into a case in the library.

He dies young — But he doesn't do that long slow terrible decay into decrepitude thing that my parents undergo. The loss of mobility and the accompanying depression. The weight gain. My father gets to the point where he can't fit into any of his Brooks Brothers suits and that's what kills him — not the broken hip. My mother gets so fat and so arthritic that she hates to move, and not moving is what kills *her*. Embolism, the docs say, but she just freezes into position and dies there.

At what point do you just want to soar out of your balloon body like Tamara's mom does in that great poem?

It's better than not being able to walk or fit into your swanky outfits.

When Louis drops dead at 60 I hope that right before he keels over he looks up and around and sees the skyline and the trees of the park.

I hope he imagines calling his mom, the way my roommate says he always did when he was sick. "Mom," he says. "Mom, it's me. I'm dying."

And then he'll float on over those famous, illuminated Central Park trees.

*The way Jamie tells it (or the way I remember it), the dog is with him, but in that case, what happens to the dog? (this would be a whole separate poem)

Two Hiking Poems

I hike Big Sur by myself, 1996
(Big Sur, California)

Not the hard trails. The easy ones. The ones with views and the ones with twisted oaks and the ones which bridge over brooks and streams, if there's a difference between those two types of water; there must be. The trails with redwoods whose trunks gape open and the daughter — if she were there — could hide in them.

It was hot and I was tired, but I knew I could handle the sharp grade and the heat. I sat on the high bench and looked at the valley.

I ate a sandwich. I drank water.

I knew needing no one was an illusion, but it was an illusion I held close that day.

I took one slow step then another going down. My legs worked; my knees worked. I stopped and rubbed my hands on a tree trunk.

The husband said I would like Big Sur. He was right, but I wasn't talking to him. I lifted my chin.

I was empty of love but it felt like survival.

I walked off the trail, saw the parking lot teeming with people.

All strangers. I felt ferocious, unrecognized. I stalked toward my car.

Hiking above Timken Road and seeing a Mountain Lion, 1997

(Anaheim Hills, California)

I keep looking to escape this racist suburb
Where they told me at the Ralph's to go back where I came
From despite the fact that I'm a white upper-class professor —
Today I found this trail
Above my house where supposedly the Wells Fargo
Stagecoach rode. My guidebook says there were robbers
Awaiting the wagons here on this ridge. But
There's nothing here, and as usual it's
Hot as hell and dry. I am moving through the ruined burnt grass
Of Orange County disappointment til
I meet the eye of something. Gold like the grass. Big.
We look at each other. We both walk
In the same direction for a while, then the gold cat turns away.
Moves sinuous muscles. I phone my parents to tell them.
I think they'll be impressed.
No!
They say "don't ever
Walk there again."
I hang up and wonder why they never have confidence in my
Ability to survive situations.
I determine
To go back to that trail tomorrow.

But I never see the mountain lion again.
Still, I dream every so often of
Burnt grasses and
Oversized
Wheels. A golden eye glares out
Between the spokes.

Before and After, 1998
(New York and Los Angeles)

Before I moved
West I saw sky in daggered slivers
Edged out by the skyscrapers, and a big expanse
Scared me. Now I go to New York and love the
Concrete canyons but soon they close
In, and I want to break out and feel that
Enormity — swim in that big open again.
In LA sometimes I go and stand on
My front porch so I can see the blue darken over
The El Royale Apartments. Mae West lived there,
And so did a bunch of other stars so they could
Be close to the studio, but I think they liked most
Being in that bowl that is Los Angeles, just north of Wilshire
looking north
And seeing the Hollywood Hills, and above all that
Still — although it's a big city — you can see so much
sky.

Commutation, 2005
(Metrolink LA-Riverside [for Brian Brophy])

it's dark as hell at
5 am,
and it's a sharp cold, which is confusing
 because this is Los Angeles.
I stagger up, try to drink some coffee.
I know it will be hot later when the sun
rises in Riverside so I pile jacket on top of sweater on top of sweater
on top of sleeveless shirt.
I put bags in the cold car.
I put my coffee in the cold car.
I drive to the train station with
the seat warmer on knowing my husband
will tease me about this choice when he
hears me tell about it later.
I go stand on the platform and it's
cold and disconnected early morning quiet, til the guy who
is an actor who teaches where I teach
says hi to me and begins imitating
the gestures of everyone waiting silently for the train.

   he shines hot sun energy despite the darkness
while I shiver at him wondering where that power
comes from when all I can do is remember — regret —
that I left my coffee when I parked the car.

I wish I could sip as I consider the actor
because he's really good and I know already
though it will take years — that I will write about him
and this unseasonable moment.

War, 2015
(Larchmont Village, Los Angeles, California)

There's a war here on the two
Fences— my neighbor's and mine — between the squirrels and
The birds.
It's been going on for days.
The two squirrels — one big one little
Mount an attack on a tree — why?
No idea. There's some weird fruit maybe
Or maybe it's existential — the tree is there
And therefore we must attack it and the bird
What kind? No idea, I am a city person and this
Is a city poem so get off my back about sub-species
And breeds — so anyhow the bird flies after them
Attacking and flapping and pecking til they both
Run back across the fences and hide under the part
Of the roof that is higher, and so makes a little
Bomb shelter for them. I feel sorry for the squirrels at
First but they recover from the pecking and they crawl
Back along the fence to attack the tree again. They
Look like soldiers, they *are* soldiers on a mission
And I wonder if there's any way out of this — attacks and counter
Attacks and the wounded licking their tails under buildings.
I wonder if my neighbor notices. Probably not.
Since his wife left him, he isn't home much. I see him

At the coffee shop with other neighbors whom I
Recognize but don't know personally. I never
Saw/heard the neighbor and his wife fighting, but one time I heard her
Orgasming alone with the windows open. He
Had gone to work. Just her car in the garage.
It sounded happy. She was glad I think to finally
Have a moment's
Peace.

On Wilshire, 2016
(Los Angeles)

I want to talk to you about the growl of garbage trucks. Comforting. How the footsteps of someone walking on the second floor feels like noisy angels moving the furniture of paradise. Yes, there's a dog up there too, skittering. A big dog by the sound of it, but nimble. I want you to feel how the gardeners violating code and using the leaf blower at 7 am is a kind of symphony of irritation but even that tells you that you are not alone and there are all kinds of unseen daimons doing all kinds of stuff in your neighborhood. You venture outside and see them: the taco truck handlers eyeballing the placement of said vehicle because it has to be situated exactly right so as to a), enable customers to approach the window, and b) not piss off the other food truck parkers by taking up too much space in the back. Then there's the guy in torn jeans and a ragged beard getting on the wilshire bus and wishing everyone a happy valentine's day. He's a spirit of benevolence and now you know that seraphim don't always wear white. I want you to know how this littered city street, counts as the "great out of doors" too, and there's nature here also although it's not babbling brooks and serene mountains. It's palm trees and mourning doves calling over the gardeners. There's a seagull flying past the rainbow that's emerged over the tarpits. And there are people going wow wow wow as the gull climbs up that rainbow, everyone taking pictures with their phones, every single person, graced by their collective amazements. And then the sunset careening brilliant pink over the alley. The cracks in the pavement jutting determined blades of grass. The trees on the verge of blooming.

Downsizing was a mistake and we ended up building a whole other section of the house but that's another story, 2016
(Coupeville, Washington)

We were trying to think
Small house
We wouldn't need closets
We'd share an office
We didn't need a laundry room
At least
We didn't skimp
On the shower
Which is the biggest
Thing in the house now
I look at my blue willow dishes
And 3 closets full of clothes and
More books than the rabbi had
According to the mover
And the purse collection
And the pictures —original art
All of it beautiful
And I
Wonder
Where

Am I

Going to

Put

It all where

Am

I

Going

To

Put

My

Sel

f

Beulah, 2017
(Coupeville, Washington)

Fact: Beulah stepped in a hole
in her neighbor's yard.

Question: why was the hole there?

Answer: the neighbors were making some kind of improvement
To the yard
but what they were doing
is not clear from B's story.

Question: what were the circumstances of the accident?

Answer: Beulah was at a barbecue.
She walked out the front door.
She walked through the yard.
That's when the accident happened.

The relevant points are:
It was night and it was dark and
The hole was narrow and deep
just big enough to step in and
fall over in
just small enough to
break what falls into it.

Aftermath: Beulah broke her foot in several
different places.
The neighbors felt bad.
It took Beulah 3 years to get mad
at them about it. And 5 no 6 surgeries — say
did you know that you've got more
bones in your feet than anywhere else
except your hands?

Current status: Beulah's foot still
doesn't work right. She sits up at night

With her painkiller and wonders: Why didn't the
neighbors fence the hole or at least
warn people not to walk in the front yard
what about a little pennant or flag? —
nope — they just figured no one would
walk there.
But Beulah walks everywhere
or at least she did
til she went over to visit those neighbors

carrying a rhubarb pie that must have been: delicious.

Have you seen? 2017
(Coupeville, Washington)

"My dog?"
A white guy pulls up in a truck.
The poet adjusts her straw hat. Is he
Some horny senior citizen trying to pick her
Up like the bearded man last summer, who drove
Next to her for 10 minutes while she was
Walking telling her about life on the island and how crazy his
First wife was? He was so broken

Down old that it took her
9 minutes to realize that this was indeed a pickup
Attempt. So, this time she's ready. But no, this man
Is looking for his golden-haired retriever. "She's really friendly"
He keeps on saying. Then — "I live over there at the place
With the fence." Poet says "I'm your neighbor." She points in
The direction of her house.
No reaction. "What's your name?" she says.
"Gary." He doesn't ask who she is. "My dog" he says. "My dog."
"I'll keep an eye out," Poet says wondering how she'll
Ever reach him if she sees the dog because he hasn't
Said his address or given her any information
Other than that he has a fence, but then so do several people.
She watches to see what driveway he pulls into.

She walks to the end of the road and turns around.

Then she sees a different (slightly younger) white man in shorts standing by

His mailbox. "Did you lose a dog?" He says. She says "no

But Gary did." "Who's he?" says Shorts.

"He's your next-door neighbor" answers

Poet.

"Well, tell him I have his dog."

Poet walks back, sees Gary in his truck. Flags him down.

"That guy down there has your dog" she informs him.

Gary guns the engine.

Suddenly a (white) woman with a shiny silver necklace runs out of Gary's driveway. "Have you seen our dog?"

"No," says Poet for the 3rd time, "but YOUR NEIGHBOR HAS." Necklace looks blank then says

"He's so upset." Meaning, the poet thinks,

Gary.

Poet walks home, pours a glass of wine

Remembers her Big East Coast City mother

Observing in an overcrowded subway car packed with silent sweaty strangers: "You know, people can be really

Weird."

Anti-Pastoral 1, 2018
(Coupeville, Washington)

1.

Nature you are a pain in the ass the way you rain every time I want to go for a walk. The silence of the deer in heat is deafening. Then there's the cawing of the birds and the monotony of trees giving oxygen, cleaning the air. "Green is boring," Tim Hatch once told me at a reading in San Dimas, and I laughed because IT'S TRUE.

2.

Everyone here sighs "it's paradise" and I respond, "Where's the Macy's?" It's not that I don't like flowers but come on — they're not everything and anyway it's not why we left our little caves looking to invent something that wasn't just wood and water and stone and bone.

2b.

The deer *eat* all the flowers here anyway.

2c.

Also, there is no recycling here and the garbage is piling up at the dump. NOT cool.

3.

Point of information: Jean Jacques Rousseau was not born in the country and Thoreau had supplies brought in, which Emerson mostly paid for. Jean Jacques wrote about natural man, but he sure beat the hell out of Geneva as soon as he could, and he lived in fancy ass Paris and London — probably so he could complain about them.

4.

I complained about the city too when we lived there. So, we moved to the country and now I miss the aggravation: the neighbors screaming, the lights going off, and the helicopters circling at 4 am. Alexander Pope wrote a poem once about a woman looking over her vast country estate. "Odious odious trees," she says.

4b.

I wouldn't go that far but what I wouldn't do for a taco truck and a dry cleaner I could walk to. Even the gurgling splat of someone spitting in the cruddy street. The spitter mutters things, and then the bus comes, and you get on behind them, but you hang back just a smidge, in case they resolve to toss another loogie. Your coins sweat slightly in your already smudged palm.

5.

The rain finally stops and the workmen arrive to repair the roof because a pine tree fell on it, right over the bedroom. It could have just driven through like a javelin. We're lucky not to be dead the tree expert tells us. One tree workman is very handsome. He sits in his truck with his blond hair and eats a sandwich. He tells me he goes fishing on the weekends. I look at my husband sitting at his computer crunching code in his bathrobe and think I've made the right choice. I mean fishing? Honestly.

Anti-Pastoral 2, 2019
(Coupeville, Washington)

Not because nature is beautiful
But because it is necessary.

Not because I am a part of it
But because I am defiantly separate, a metropolitan alien.

Not because I love it — not from any affection
But because I need to breathe air that won't kill me.

Not because the flowers bloom (they don't because the deer devour
them down to the roots)
But because dirt grows things I want to eat.

Not because of hikes and trails and kayaks on water
But because eagles live here now, soaring back from the promised
extinction.

Not because of pristine forests which let's face it are the scary locus
of fairy tales
But because of shrines tucked into them lined with stones — secret
churches made by the homeless youth that camp out here. As
young as 12. As young as 10.

Not because of rods and tackle and those ghastly fish wriggling on
their death-hooks

But because of living orcas I have never seen.

Not because nature's great and spiritual

But because my mother said "practically, we need it." She lived in
small apartments her entire life and positively hated bees.

For the window cleaner March 22nd 2021
(Whidbey Island)

Every man here reminds me of
My father – that's it! That's the
Problem with living on this island
Paradise – everyone is protestant
Pissed off and white, disappointed
By higher taxes, enraged by government
Offices. And just plain mad. Mad about
The money that didn't accrue, mad about the kids,
Who've moved away looking for jobs
On the mainland
Mad about
How everything takes time and effort
And even though you're handsome
Or think you are, time drags on you, the lines form
And things sag. The Puget Sound possessions: the
Boat, the jet skis, and even the fishing rod demand
Constant care and tending, and soon it'll all need to
Be replaced, and so here you are washing windows
Of these big houses in Langley or even here on Madrona
These big flipping houses and what did these people do
To deserve them? Nothing or else everything or else they
Were just lucky, and so they get to come here in the summer
And go to Arizona in the winter.

It goes like that, I think, their anger, and it's a reminder
I suppose that suffering doesn't build character
Sadness doesn't make you better, kinder, more patient
Rather it's that constant swipe of the squeegie on glass
The clean that doesn't stay, because things are declining
And there's so much more to do. The pine needles falling
Everywhere, and on the road to the next job
you need to swerve continually to avoid
Hitting a deer.

Eva Gabor encourages the poet to take a break from the country in the guise of Lisa Douglas from *Green Acres* with adjectives taken out and every other line erased per a Bernadette Mayer prompt, timeless
(*en route*)

Darling — Give me the city, rather than this emergency of evergreenery
With these neighbors — all identically —
there *you* are with makeup, bras, manifestos
Sans cleaner, florist, taco-truck, pho kiosk, subway, bus OR taxi—
You moisturize, catch up on
the owls with your stock of wine.
It won't help.
You'll need a room in a city,
Someone spitting on pavement —
A Dollar Store. An opera. Sephora. Sirens. Yelling.
You'll get grounded by noise.
Believe me, heaven is. It's hell that's.
Don't beat yourself up about being a cityslicker —
Even Joni Mitchell
Lives in LA now. She knows where the doctors are and that there's
Supermarket delivery.

People *aren't* in the country.
Remember how you stood at that bus stop for hours, waiting til it dawned
The route was changed? No one stopped.

So, forget it —
Take a plane
Just
Don't
Flip pancakes in a
Negligee while you climb
A pole to answer
The phone.

SoCal you are my country, 2019
(North Hollywood, California [for Lillian Behrendt and Robert Murphy])

SoCal you are my country
Where I worked at the bankrupt university
Where I birthed books, my favorite human
An almost divorce,
And at least two nervous breakdowns.
It's too hot to live here
The allergens kill me
The drought's over only for now
But I see those too tall palm trees
Shimmering in the 100-degree temperature
Waving in front of the too big building
On Lankershim
And I feel the power pouring into me
From the heat. There's songs and stories
Still left in me. They rise up like sweet young things
Strutting their stuff on Chandler and Ventura in high heels
Flexing tattooed muscles bending back barbells in a Burbank gym
Dreaming of fake fights under television cameras.
Those orange buses keep lumbering around the corner
And they will take me somewhere beach-like and surprising
Or even hotter than this spot. It's possible.
Agoura Hills maybe or even Pacoima.

See — I'd rather burn up here alive and
Smoldering
Than dissolve in the moisture of those
Admittedly beautiful pacific northwest trees.
Understand — I hate some of the people here
More than any I've known anywhere
But the ones I love most are also here
In Beverly Hills, Ontario, Echo Park, Venice,
Riverside, Claremont, Westwood — and right here
In North Hollywood
Along with
Comic books
Nudie Cohn informational plaques
Broken down small theaters
Garage bands and symphonies
And galleries showing paintings by background painters
For the major studios. Funny how what they paint in
Their spare time —
That's all backgrounds too.
Like me, I'm a background poet. What's
Cool about being in the background is you can
Focus
On whatever you want.
Like eating. I'm hungry now and
My feet tread the sizzling pavement

For a pizza, and then a coffee. At the Starbucks I take
A picture of 3 men who were at some studio
Function. They're friends. They want a memento of being
All dressed up in tuxes getting iced coffees.
"Smile," I say, "it's balmy."
And the guy in the Ray Bans says, "Wow —sweetie, that's a
really pretty, unusual

    Name."

City slicker, 2019
(New York City)

I can ride backward in trains
I can stand up on buses
I can walk like I know where I'm going and I'm going there fast
I can apply lipstick without a mirror
I can find the ladies lounge in any department store
I am always fashion forward even when broke
I can eat a hotdog with sauerkraut and cross the street.
without spilling
and if I trip it'll look fantastic —
traffic lights are merely a suggestion for pedestrians —
I always cross in the middle of the block anyway.
I am 25 when
I learn how to drive
in North Carolina because why bother?
I like crowds and
waiting in line for the perfect slice of pizza .
I don't know the names of trees
but I dig their barkiness
and grass and flowers
dogs on leashes
birds on patios and pavement.

I like hair salons and paintings and

cathedrals, and synagogues—

sit with me at the counter of this chipped coffee shop and tell me
the stories you've overheard on the subway or the bus or

on the corner

or through the walls of the bathroom — say

what did the lovers whisper

as they brushed their urbanized teeth?

Acknowledgments

"Beulah" and "Have you Seen" appeared originally in *Literary Alchemy*, volume 2, issue 1.

"Night in 5" appeared originally in *Hole in The Head*. Issue 22.

"Anti-Pastoral 1" and "Pine Cones" appeared originally in *Red Shift* 4.

"Outside at Night" appeared originally in *SHARK REEF* literary magazine. Issue 29.

"For the Window Cleaner" originally appeared in *25 Miles from Here*.

"War" originally appeared in the *Cultural Weekly*, September 11th, 2019.

About the Author

Stephanie Barbé Hammer is a 6-time Pushcart Prize nominee in fiction, nonfiction and poetry with work published in *The Bellevue Literary Review, Hayden's Ferry Review, Pearl, the James Franco Review, Isthmus, Cafe Irreal,* and *the Gold Man Review.*

She is the author of the prose poem chapbook SEX WITH BUILDINGS (dancing girl press), the full-length collection HOW FORMAL? (Spout Hill Press), the fabulist novel THE PUPPET TURNERS OF NARROW INTERIOR (Urban Farmhouse Press), and the craft of writing magical realism manual, DELICIOUS STRANGENESS (Spout Hill Press).

Originally from Manhattan, Stephanie lived in Southern California for 30 years. She is managing editor of SHARK REEF Literary Magazine and sits on the advisory board of WRITERS BLOC Los Angeles.

Also from Bamboo Dart Press
by Stephanie Barbé Hammer

Rescue Plan (2021)

In the New England town of Narrow Interior, 15 year old cancer survivor Gomer Faithcutt prepares for the practical Junior Life Saving Test while exploring both his own sexuality and the spectral secrets of a forgotten religious sect that once flourished in the town. As his father worries about his son's health, Gomer learns about desire, friendship, and self-preservation. He glimpses who he can become because of (or despite?) his parents and forges a surprising connection with a mysterious neighbor.

BAMBOO
DART
PRESS

112 N. Harvard Ave. #65
Claremont, CA 91711
chapbooks@bamboodartpress.com
www.bamboodartpress.com

www.ingramcontent.com/pod-product-compliance
Lightning Source LLC
Chambersburg PA
CBHW081241020426
42331CB00013B/3252